American Hero Day

by Alice Cary
Illustrated by Barbara Kiwak

PEARSON

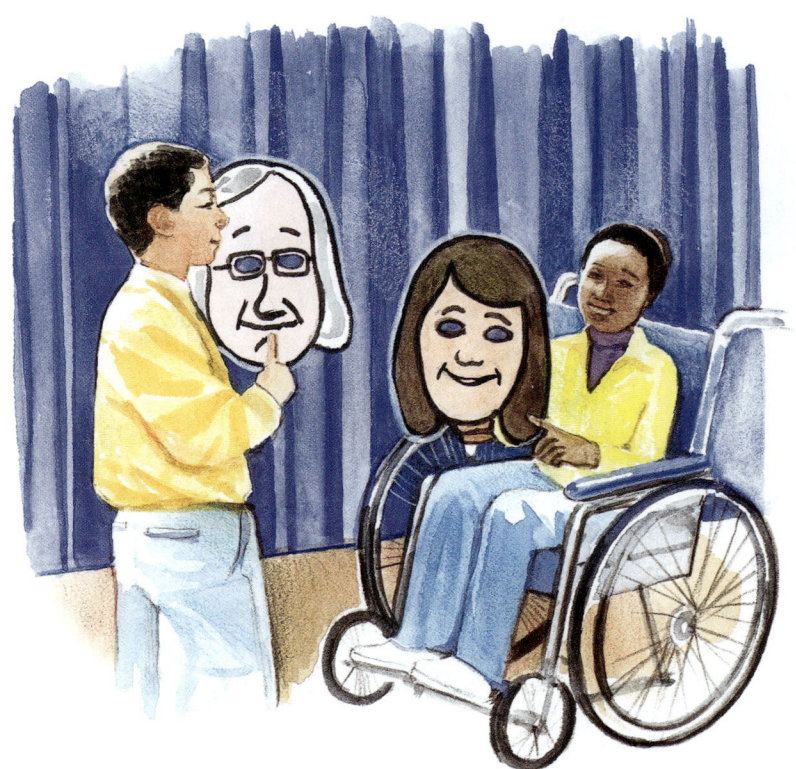

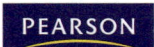

Glenview, Illinois • Boston, Massachusetts • Chandler, Arizona
Upper Saddle River, New Jersey

It is American Hero Day!
Mr. Brown's class makes masks.
A cat steps in paint.
The cat runs on the masks.
"What a mess!" says Mr. Brown.

"What can we do?" asks Jin.
"The show is tonight."
"We can paint new masks,"
says Mary.
"There is no time," says Mr. Brown.

"Baker School has an American Hero Day too," says Carlos. "Maybe we can borrow their masks."
"That is a great idea!" says Mr. Brown.

Mr. Brown calls Mrs. Clay.
"May we borrow your masks?"
"Of course you can!" says Mrs. Clay.
"Mrs. Clay is our hero," says Mary.

The parents come to school.
The show begins.
The children wear the masks.

Mary is Sally Ride.
Sally Ride was the first American woman in space.
Greg is the first President, George Washington.

Everyone loves the show.
The parents clap.
"Carlos had a great idea," says Mary.
"He is our hero today."